A GARDENER'S DICTIONARY

gardening

A GARDENER'S DICTIONARY

BY HENRY BEARD
& ROY McKIE

WORKMAN PUBLISHING
NEW YORK

Library of Congress Cataloging in Publication Data

Beard, Henry.
    Gardening: a dictionary for weedpullers, slugcrushers, and
    backyard botanists.

    1. Gardening—Dictionaries—Anecdotes, facetiae, satire, etc.
    2. Gardening—Anecdotes, facetiae, satire, etc. I. McKie,
    Roy. II. Title.
SB455.B38   635'.0207   81-43783
ISBN 0-89480-201-1   AACR2
ISBN 0-89480-200-3 (pbk.)

Produced by Edward T. Riley
Art Director: Paul Hanson
Designer: Geoffrey Stevens
Workman Publishing Company
1 West 39 Street
New York, New York 10018

Manufactured in the United States of America

First printing April 1982

10 9 8 7 6 5

To all those who have heard the call of the land.

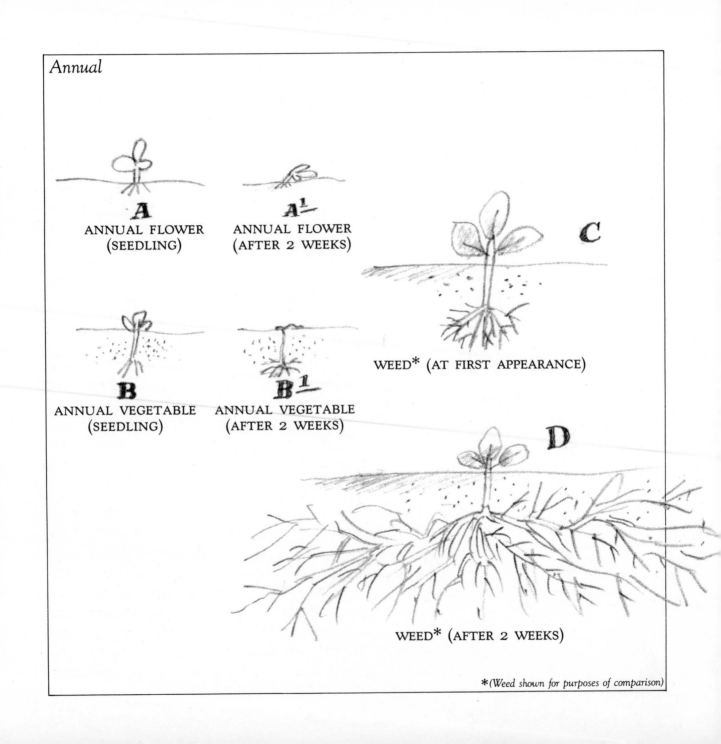

Annual

A
ANNUAL FLOWER
(SEEDLING)

A¹
ANNUAL FLOWER
(AFTER 2 WEEKS)

B
ANNUAL VEGETABLE
(SEEDLING)

B¹
ANNUAL VEGETABLE
(AFTER 2 WEEKS)

C
WEED* (AT FIRST APPEARANCE)

D
WEED* (AFTER 2 WEEKS)

(Weed shown for purposes of comparison)

A

Annual	Any plant that dies before blooming. *See* PERENNIAL.
Annual Rings	The age of a tree can be exactly determined by cutting through the trunk horizontally and counting the concentric rings that mark each separate season's growth. Unfortunately, this method entails a very severe trade-off between precise knowledge and the continued health of the specimen examined.
Aphid	Insect pest that inphests gardens and makes gardeners phoam at the mouth, stamp their pheet, and utter phour-letter words.
Arbor Day	The last Friday in April is the "birthday" of many trees. If your property boasts a number of fine specimens, you really should "take them out to dinner" with a good root-feeding of essential nutrients. If you want to splurge on a gift as well, you might consider one of those nice etched plastic plates that give the tree's proper botanical name, a gypsy moth trap, a tasteful birdhouse, or some attractively tailored burlap trunk wrap.
Arboretum	Basically a zoo for plants and trees. Although not as exciting as their counterparts that display members of the animal kingdom, arboretums and botanical gardens are much more easygoing. For example, plant-keepers rarely object if children feed the trees a little potassium, and even the largest and most ill-tempered species can do little more than drop a nut on your head or slough off a dead branch or two into your path. And as for their by-products—well, no one ever complains about getting oxygen on their shoes!

Arranging Flowers	Thanks to the tireless work of many talented ladies and dedicated garden clubs, flower arranging has been transformed from a hobby into an art. Nevertheless, the novice should not be daunted by the apparent complexity of it all. Success is guaranteed if one always keeps in mind that, whether the arrangement is to be presented in a formal show or in an informal house setting, the goals one should be aiming to achieve are: envy, grudging praise, and imitation by rivals. Always strive to avoid giggles, whispers, and catty remarks. This basic principle applies regardless of which of the four contemporary flower arranging styles one chooses to specialize in: Traditional Vulgar Bulk Display Supported by Wire and Space Age Glues; Casual Country Massing in Conversation Piece Procured During Travel in Fancy Places; Aggressive Oriental Understatement with Big Rocks, a Single Branch, and Well-memorized Chinese Double-talk; or Abstract Presentation of Something Odd and Costly from Hawaii in a Container Designed for the Transport of Radioactive Substances.
Artichoke	The only vegetable as troublesome to eat as it is to grow.
Asparagus	Delectable vegetable often planted because its very short season makes commercial varieties a scarce item in stores. It's one of the most problematic vegetables around, since it must be placed in soil dug to a considerable depth, and the stalks are either blighted by rust, don't come up at all, or must be left to develop the following year's crop. But many gardeners plant asparagus anyway, probably for the satisfaction of having it unavailable in their own gardens several weeks before it is unobtainable in the local market.
Autumn	Delightful season that runs from the disposal of the last zucchini to the arrival of the first catalog.

Avocado

As a bonus in every avocado, nature includes a "free" houseplant—a large, inedible nut which, if balanced over a glass of water on toothpicks until it develops root hairs, and then potted, will eventually become an uninteresting 2- or 3-foot tall plant that will never bear fruit. It is estimated that there are 70 million avocado plants in the U.S., a staggering glut that stems from a widespread belief that a law similar to the one which prohibits the removal of furniture tags from sofa cushions forbids the disposal of the avocado pit. *There is no such law. You may discard all your avocado plants immediately.* (If you find you have trouble doing so, contact your local chapter of Avocadon't, a very worthwhile organization that has helped thousands of people enslaved by this insidious plant.)

B

Bayberry

In colonial times, the bayberry was an important source of wax for candles, and in spite of immense technological progress since then, it is still a financially significant plant, playing a vital role in the $800-million colonial gift shop business. Observers have long lamented the reliance of this key industry on a single plant, and their warnings proved prophetic when a disastrous harvest in 1976 cut bayberry candle, soap, and sachet production in half. It is generally felt that but for the huge sales of fake parchment Declarations of Independence during the Bicentennial, many shops would have closed. There has subsequently been some diversification into needlework and pewter, but the nation is still dangerously dependent on the fickle bayberry.

Beach Plum

1. Bothersome seashore fruit that may be converted with considerable effort into a bland jelly. *2.* Attractive, scantily clad young lady on the beach who may be observed at fairly close range while pretending to pick *1.*

Bed

1. Where most prized flowering perennials are located. *2.* Where most gardeners are located when they hear rabbits in *1.*

Bee

Generic name for any of a number of stinging insects, most commonly the honeybee. Contrary to popular belief, bees almost never sting, unless they are mating, feeding, resting, swarming, leaving the hive, or returning to the hive.

Beech

Nurseryman's technical term for either: *1.* A very difficult landscaping job or *2.*, A woman supervising such a job.

Berry

Small fruit produced by a variety of flowering bushes and shrubs, some wild, some cultivated. Most are edible and delicious, but a few are extremely toxic. How can you tell them apart? There is an easy rule of thumb: Look for telltale "clustering" in a pale green or gray cardboard box with a cellophane covering and a distinctive reddish rubber band. Berries with those features are always safe to eat.

Birch

The list of the ten most common ornaments in American front yards is headed by the canoe birch, whose dazzling white bark is much prized. The rest of the list: blue spruce, dwarf red Japanese maple, Lombardy poplar, animal figurines, religious statuettes, gnomes, jockeys, shiny globes on pedestals, and yucca plants.

Blight

General term for a plant disease that simultaneously kills all members of a single species in any given area. The chestnut blight and Dutch elm disease are the two best known and

Birch (Obscured by Other Lawn Ornaments)

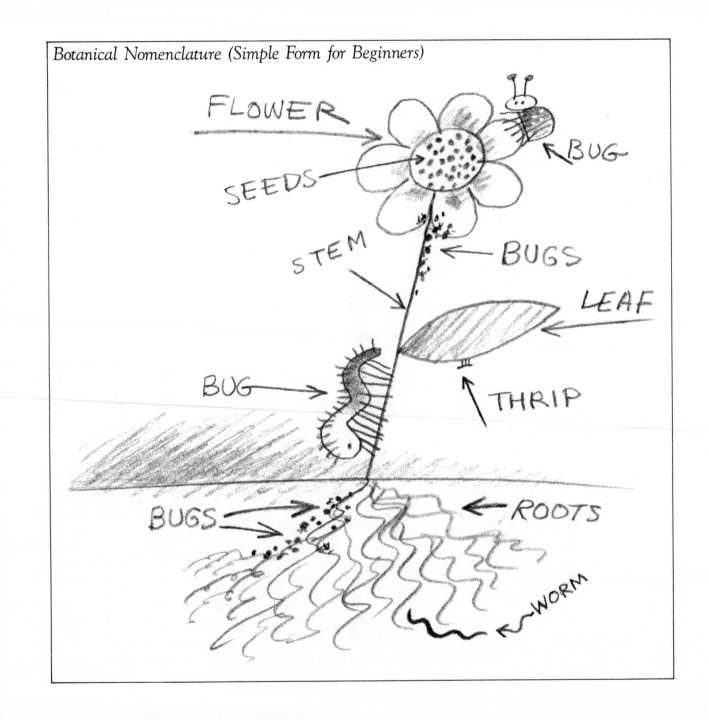

Botanical Nomenclature (Simple Form for Beginners)

most tragic examples. Despite years of effort by chemists, botanists, and biologists, no practical method of protecting these two magnificent trees or of breeding truly immune varieties has ever been found. On a somewhat brighter note, however, a good deal of progress *is* being made on the development of a blight that will devastate canoe birches, blue spruces, dwarf red Japanese maples, Lombardy poplars, and most forms of yucca.

Bluegrass	Rare lawn condition in which normally brown, crisp lawns develop odd patches of a sort of hazy green growth. Don't be alarmed! These strangely colored areas usually disappear within a few weeks.
Bonsai	The Japanese art of dwarfing trees to produce tiny, picturesque specimens is growing in popularity in the U.S. On the other hand, the somewhat more demanding art of miniature forestry (*bunyu*) has yet to catch on, perhaps because the only reward for the skill involved in the manipulation of the tiny chain saws, matchbox-size logging trucks, and minute lumber mills is a reliable source of inexpensive toothpicks.
Border	Strip of ground that divides the area where the shrubs were from the place where the lawn will be with a neat row of white plastic markers indicating where the flowers would have been.
Botanical Nomenclature	The system currently in use for naming plants is based on one devised by a Swedish botanist known variously as Carl Linne, Carl von Linne, and Carolus Linnaeus, whose confusion over his own name has unfortunately extended to his system. The initial two words under the Linnaean system are always Latin. (Ideally, they shouldn't "give away"

what the plant is or be easy to say or spell—that spoils the fun!) The first word describes the species of the plant, the second the particular individual. Thus, if some horticultural investigator turned up a new thick-stemmed orchid with flowers shaped like a shoe, it might be named *Chyrrhaemzygophylla braeiourhynspsia*, which may be abbreviated to *C. braeiourhynspsia*. (Plants are sometimes named after their discoverer, but the authorities responsible for the designations are reluctant to do this unless the botanist to be honored has a very peculiar name, like O'Clytemnestra or Ffrench-Turpsichert.) Following these two Latin words, a third sometimes appears indicating the variety of the plant if it has some particular quality others lack, as for example, that it is unusually difficult to grow *(irascibilia)*, has a noticeable odor *(phooeyii)*, or looks like something fell on it *(obliterata)*. Now, if a particular specimen develops, say, brilliant red blossoms instead of the tiny white ones it displays in the wild, it might be further qualified as a cultivar and have an additional epithet, preceded by the letters *c.v.*, like *"Carmine Miranda."* Many nurseries contribute to the confusion by applying their own names to plants, like "Flame of the Amazon—the Rarest Orchid in the World!" or "Cobra Breath—Snatched from the Jaws of South American Serpents!" and as a result most gardeners rely on the simpler Universal Plant Identification Code, under which *C. braeiourhynspsia* is "That Thick-stemmed Orchid with Flowers Shaped Like a Shoe in the Green Pot."

Broccoli	Member of the cabbage family grown chiefly as receptacle for Hollandaise sauce.
Brochures and Catalogs	Forms of entertaining fiction published by nurseries, seedsmen, and tool manufacturers.

Bugs (The Thrip)

Broom

Pleasant blooming plant from some varieties of which (chiefly Scotch broom) house brooms were once made by our pioneer ancestors. Gardens were a source of many other equally useful household items in those simpler, less troubled times. For example, dried lima beans were often used as bullets; vines, particularly bittersweet, were made into handcuffs and garrotes; and winter squashes, hollowed out and filled with gunpowder and bits of seashell or chestnut burrs, served as reliable homespun grenades.

Brussels Sprouts

This relative of the cabbage was thought in medieval times to be a source of "fetid humors" and was dubbed "the devil's hell-ball." The plant was officially declared anathema in Pope Boniface VII's bull of 1304 ("De Gustibus Detestabilis"), and for several centuries thereafter the offending vegetable was actively suppressed, and any wild specimens that appeared were publicly roasted in town squares on the feast day of St. Fenton of Bruges. Alas, this practice has become rare in the general drift away from traditional religious customs.

Bugs

There are a variety of methods of controlling insects, but—let's be honest—they just don't work. Why not "rock with the punch" so to speak and establish an insect garden? Although a bed of slugs or a curving border of shimmering Japanese beetles may not be as spectacular as more traditional plantings, and a centerpiece of grubs and larvae on the dining table might be a little alarming, you will have the peace of mind that comes from never having to worry that a sudden infestation of cabbages will kill your prize loopers, or that radishes will attack your thrips, or that a peach tree will get your borers.

Burl

The usual method of preparing vegetables.

C

Cactus

Millions of years of adaptation to brutal desert conditions have made this family of plants ideal for the lazy gardener, since there is very little for him or her to do between purchasing the plant and discarding it (anywhere from a week to fifty years later), except to knock it over from time to time and break its pot.

Carrot

Crunchy, root vegetable the consumption of which is alleged to improve eyesight. The veracity of this folk belief is challenged to some degree by the large number of rabbit cadavers on streets and highways.

Catnip

Widely planted herb that produces a powerful narcotic effect on cats, probably similar to the effect of cannabis on humans. One pound of the weed typically has an "alley value" of eight to ten mice.

Celery

Practically no one grows this plant for his or her own consumption, but gardeners can pick up a few extra dollars raising it and several other kinds of produce for the restaurant industry, which uses millions of tons annually as *garni* and in salad bars. Best bets are: celery itself, of course, principally the fibrous, hard-stemmed "Ghastly Snack"; beets, particularly "Steam Table" and "Alcatraz"; and any of the new varieties of iceberg lettuce, including "Lunch Leather" and "Dish Debris."

Christmas Tree

Any well-shaped evergreen 5 to 7 feet in height situated on public land or in a remote area of private land that can be transferred from its habitat to the roof of an automobile in less than 10 minutes.

Cactus (In Transit)

Compost

Clematis	Many talented amateurs have worked to improve this unusual flowering vine, but none can compare in persistence and dedication to a pair of turn-of-the-century Americans, as this list of their successful hybrids attests:

"RUTHERFORD ANDERSON LAWRENCE." (1890) *Crimson flowers, 4–6 inches in diameter.*

"MISS LAVINIA BATEMAN." (1890) *Pearly white flowers, 2–4 inches in diameter. Long blooming.*

"MY LAVINIA." (1892) *Profuse pink flowers, 4 inches in diameter. Blooms in June.*

"DEAR MR. LAWRENCE." (1893) *Pale red flowers, 4 inches in diameter. Blooms in late May.*

"MR. AND MRS. R. A. LAWRENCE." (1894) *Pink flowers, 4–6 inches in diameter. Very fragrant.*

"MISS TOODLES LaBUSTE." (1896) *Scarlet flowers, 6–8 inches in diameter. Very fragrant.*

"ATTORNEY-AT-LAW." (1896) *Tiny purple flowers. Very hardy, fast-growing vine.*

"RECONCILIATION." (1897) *Yellow flowers, 6–8 inches in diameter. Leaves and buds quite poisonous.*

"IN MEMORIAM R.A.L." (1898) WHITE FLOWERS, 6 INCHES IN DIAMETER. NO FRAGRANCE. SHORT BLOOMING PERIOD.

"CAP D'ANTIBES." (1901) *Mauve flowers, 8–10 inches in diameter. Late blooming.*

Club-Moss	Perennially present members of gardening societies.
Cold-Frame	Elaborate display case for showing off a gardener's collection of freeze-dried specimens.
Compost	Gardeners are generally quite pleasant individuals, but they often become unnecessarily graphic when discussing the constituents of the detritus of which their compost

heaps are composed. This can be annoying and disturbing for the houseguest, visitor, or dining companion, but it does carry with it the hidden bonus that the usual house gift of flowers, pastry, or wine can be dispensed with in favor of a bag of potato skins, some eggshells, or the contents of a recently cleaned cat box.

Corn

Native American cereal plant of enormous value. Its cultivation was first demonstrated to the colonists of Massachusetts Bay by friendly Indians who, in an early demonstration of the value of fertilizer, instructed the settlers to bury a dead fish in each seed mound. The colonists later greatly improved the yield and made further areas available for corn production by switching to a more intensive farming system in which a dead Indian was buried in each seed mound.

Cosmos

Large, showy flowering bush (*C. sagani*) that produces beelions and beelions of seeds.

Crab Grass

Extraordinarily tenacious garden weed. The only method of controlling it currently on the market is the lawn howitzer, a small turf mortar that fires a tapered projectile with a 10-ounce, shaped thermite charge. If the root-piercing shell strikes the plant directly at its center, it will kill the weed about half the time. The resulting crater can be turned into an attractive fishpond.

Crows

Canny birds that are rarely frightened either by dummies in the garden or dummies of dummies in the garden.

Culpability Brown

Embittered by the fame and favor enjoyed by his celebrated landscape architect twin brother Capability, who pioneered a revolution in garden design in 18th-century England, Culpability turned his warped genius to a life of botanical

crime. His devilish experiments first came to light in 1798 when a pair of moles the size of wolfhounds, who had annihilated the great lawn of a nearby estate and savaged a pair of swans in the process, were traced to his odious laboratory. On searching the premises, detectives of Scotland Yard's Root and Branch Branch discovered that the mad horticulturist was on the verge of producing a successful cross between a stinging nettle and a copper beech and was breeding a variety of termite with a taste for croquet sets. Briefly imprisoned, he was released after agreeing to go into exile. Little is known of his life after that, but there are clues to his wanderings: In 1801, an incredibly effective passenger pigeon bird call became available in the U.S., and in 1809 a foreigner visiting Kyoto persuaded an imperial gardener to accept, as a gift, a pair of starlings, asking in return only a pound or two of Japanese beetles.

Cultivation	The only sure method of removing weeds is by "working the soil" with fork, spade, or hoe to loosen the roots. With stubborn weeds, however, it's best to "live and let live" and simply label the offending plant with its Latin name and modestly accept compliments on its robust growth.

D

Daisy	1. Ubiquitous wild flower with target-shaped blossoms. 2. Popular brand of air rifle used by offspring of gardeners to shoot heads off 1.
Damn Anemone	Perennial herb imn the buttercup fanimly with amn extremenely amnoying mname.

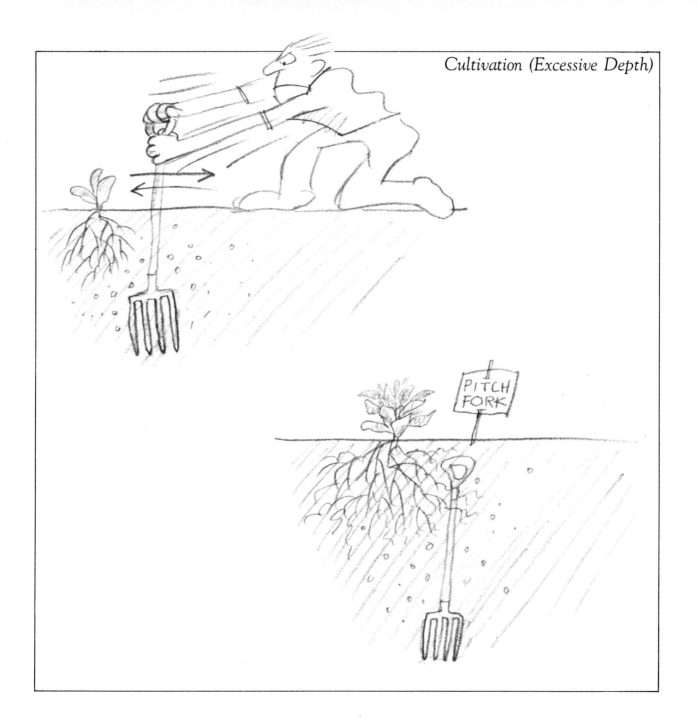

Dowsing

Dandelion The dandelion is often unfairly dismissed as nothing but a pesky weed by those who do not recognize its many uses. The leaves can be boiled to produce a green sludge that may be puréed and used to patch gutters; the flowers can be fermented into a potent, winelike beverage (or, if somewhat less sugar is added, into a homemade paint remover); the roots, cut up and roasted, can be force-fed to poultry and cats; and the fluffy seed hairs of 5,000 or so of the plants will provide a serviceable stuffing for a small toss pillow.

Dianthus Genetic term for a gardener who possesses two aunts. This condition generally results in a lack of vigor and an overall wilted look.

Delph Abbrv fr "delphinium," lg shwy prnnl w bl flrs. Othr cmmn abbrvs incl "mum," "snap," "daff," n "glad." If u cn rd ths dfntn, u cn gt a gd jb at a nrsry.

Dog The only garden pest to be successfully domesticated.

Dowsing The use of a forked twig, brass rod, or other object to locate and obtain sources of money from individuals who believe that sources of water can be located and obtained through the use of a forked twig, brass rod, or other object.

E

Eggplant Purplish, meaty vegetable whose taste when cooked—which depends considerably on the method of preparation, and there are many—has been variously compared to burnt liver, fried sandals, scorched clams, a wallet, old magazines, and mud.

Electroculture

Many homeowners—chiefly Americans of Mediterranean descent—favor a kind of "ivy" on the fronts of their houses which consists of 1,000 feet or so of extension cord punctuated by tiny bulbs. This colorful and nearly indestructible perennial creeper is usually night-blooming during much of the year. It can be killed by removing its short, pluglike root and then—and *only* then—cutting its rubbery stem in two or three inconspicuous places with a pair of insulated wire cutters to interrupt the flow of "juice." This is best done very late at night.

Espalier

A method of training trees into rigid patterns by tying their branches to wires. Now a formal gardening technique, it had its beginnings in the 14th century during one of the lengthy, polite, and nearly bloodless wars of the era of chivalry. During the investiture of Dijon in 1374, Louis IX created "Les Espaliers du Roi," a crack body of gardeners who planted young saplings along one wall of the besieged town. By the early fall of 1388, Louis' men were able to clamber easily up the ladderlike limbs and capture the city. The event marked the first appearance of organic gardening methods, since the Dijonnais had regularly pelted the Espaliers with garbage during their patient work, and the resulting compost appears to have produced, ironically, vastly improved growth. It's worth mentioning in passing that the last stand of the Espaliers—by then a purely ceremonial unit—occurred in 1789, when thirty of the valiant soldier-gardeners attempted to stop the rampaging mobs menacing Versailles by planting thorny rosebushes in their path.

Fence (Ornamental)

Experiment Stations

There is a federally supported agricultural experiment station in each of the fifty states and the Commonwealth of Puerto Rico, and these research centers are engaged in a variety of botanical projects. For example, the station in Connecticut is attempting to produce a hybrid of poison ivy that will affect only minority groups. The California station is devoting its efforts to producing a high-protein edible surfboard from pressed melon rinds and tofu. Pennsylvania is concentrating its resources on finding uses for some of the new plant species that have turned up around the damaged Three Mile Island nuclear reactor, including the tomatodendron and the fascinating "walking pumpkins." Puerto Rico is trying to produce a colorful flowering plant that can live on automobile dashboards. And Oklahoma and Texas, with some important help from the oil industry, are engaged in a joint effort to develop a fungus that will kill—or at least stunt—the jojoba bush, a very promising plant that New Mexico is working hard to improve following the discovery that its sap has lubricating qualities that could make it a substitute for the oil used in automobile and truck transmissions.

F

Fauna

Grounds keeper's term for individual not from the U.S.

Fence

Wire barrier erected to protect garden produce against animal pests that lack wings, paws, teeth, or brains, and cannot leap, tunnel, climb, or fly.

Fern

What faunas are.

Fig.	Incomprehensible illustration in gardening books.

Flower Show	Judges at flower shows use a universal point system to determine prize-winners. Familiarity with it will improve your score.

EXHIBIT:

Is not poisonous to the touch	1
Lacks thorns and spines	1
Does not cause sneezing	1
Does not produce stains and blisters	1
Appears to be alive	1
Is not a gladiolus	5
Is not a violet	5
Is not a rose	5

LUNCH:

Originality	5
Edibility	20

REFRESHMENTS:

Quality	10
Quantity	20

BONUS POINTS:

Subtlety of cash transfer	5
Firm palm contact	5
Currency folded neatly	5
Naturalness during transaction	5
Dollar amount	50

Fluorescent Light	You can grow plants under ordinary office-type fluorescent lights, but be warned—they are likely to develop odd habits: They will bloom only from about 9:00 A.M. to 5:00 P.M.; they will require a powerful mulch of paper, ashes, and coffee grounds; they will tend to cluster around water supplies; the plant heads will generally turn toward any windows or clocks and begin to droop around 3:00 P.M.;

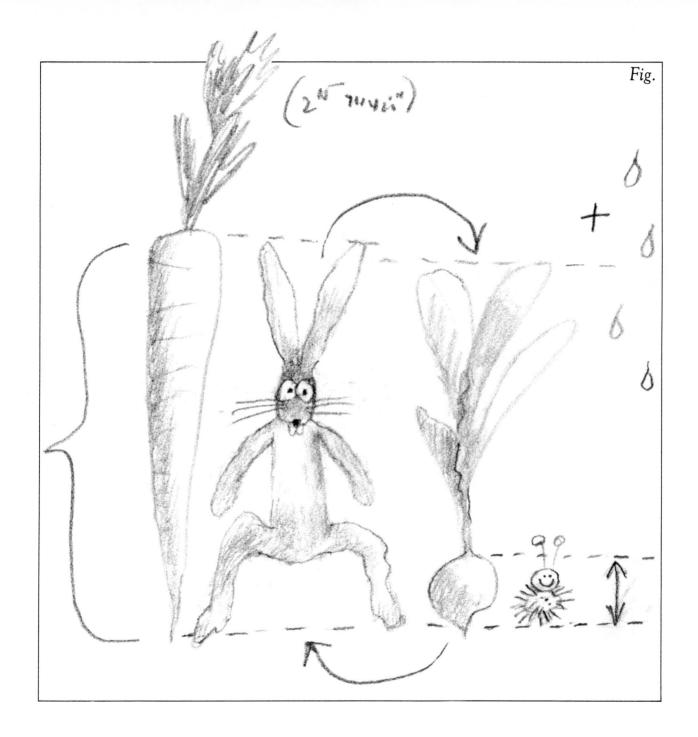

Garden

and none of the plants will ever blossom or produce any fruit.

Forcing	Most flowering tree branches and many bulbs can be forced to bloom indoors in early spring by using techniques developed in Germany and Argentina. The methods involve the use of electricity and sharp tools; the withholding of water and fertilizer; and the placement of the plant in a dark, locked room for several weeks. Forcing was condemned at the Geneva Horticultural Exposition of 1928.
Freesia	Where the excess vegetables are put.
Fruit	General term for the seed-bearing part of a plant that turns mushy, is eaten by birds or worms, drops off, rots, gets funny spots and speckles, pockmarks the lawn, isn't what was pictured in the catalog, tastes like a glove, or doesn't appear at all.
Furrow	Horizontal line on forehead of gardener. *See* HARROWING.

G

Gall	*1.* Insect or fungal infection that results in large round swollen area on leaves or twigs. *2.* Insolent attitude of visiting gardener that results in large round swollen area on lip or jaw.
Garden	One of a vast number of free outdoor restaurants operated by charity-minded amateurs in an effort to provide healthful, balanced meals for insects, birds, and animals.

Gentleman Farmer

Garden Fertilizer	The feeding of plants is a complicated and quite technical procedure, but the few essential facts about fertilizers can be quickly mastered. Just remember the numbers 3-2-5. They refer to: the three basic types—messy, stinky, and messy/stinky; the two sizes they are available in—tidbit (4-ounce packet) and blammo (220-pound sack); and the five methods of application—too much, too little, too early, too late, and wrong kind.
Gazebo!	Explosive sound produced by hay fever sufferers.
Gentleman Farmer	Individual whose major cash crop is cash, and hence whose chief agricultural pursuit consists of raising objections to the tax code.
Gin	*1.* Remarkable agricultural aid developed in the 19th century by Yankee tinkerers. *2.* Remarkable agricultural aid developed in the 18th century by British distillers.
Goldenrod	Very showy wild flower, but *ga-* unfortunately it is *ga-* a major *ga-* cause of sinus allergy *ga- ga-* among hay fever *ga-* sufferers.
Goldenrod Pollen	*Zebo!*
Gourds	Brightly colored bottle-shaped vegetables that, when dried and polished, provide decorative touches in homes in remote rural areas where lava lamps, zebra-stripe pillows, velvet paintings, and rotating mirrored balls are often unavailable. *They left out pink flamingos*
Grape	Uninteresting larval stage of wine.
Green Thumb	Common condition suffered by gardeners in which the skin of the thumb develops a greenish hue as the result of handling large amounts of currency at nurseries.

Greenhouse

Many people have found that a greenhouse provides a solace in our increasingly difficult world. A mean-spirited employer, a shrewish spouse, a persistent creditor, a meddlesome in-law—they all seem to disappear as the happy gardener putters around among his oleanders, nightshade, mistletoe, mandrake, hemlock, and foxglove, diligently crushing the glossy leaves and brightly colored berries to produce the jams and jellies for which he is justly noted or selecting from among his orchids, jasmine, camelias, and gardenias a few blossoms for the tasteful funeral sprays that garner him so much praise. In time, magically, his problems fade away, and he is left in tranquil solitude surrounded by his generous and uncomplaining botanical companions.

Ground Cover

Plants that spread easily, grow low to the ground, need little care, and do well in poor soils or shady situations are highly prized. Pachysandra, fragrant sumac, and English ivy are all widely used, although in terms of popularity in this country, nothing surpasses native American macadam or tarmac.

Ground Nut

Soil expert.

Grub

1. Beetle larva. *2.* Your lawn, from a hungry beetle larva's point of view.

Gypsy Moth

An extremely damaging insect pest that, in its caterpillar stage, is a voracious consumer of the leaves of a number of trees. All attempts at controlling it have failed. The only really successful method of dealing with a major infestation is to mix 2 ounces of gin or vodka with a dash of vermouth, place in a covered container with ice and shake vigorously. Drink the mixture. Forget the gypsy moths.

Gypsophilia

Unnatural love of gypsy moths. A very serious perversion.

H

Hardy

A plant is said to be hardy if it remains alive in a nursery long enough to be sold.

Harrowing

Type of gardening experience that produces furrows.

Harvest

For most amateur gardeners, the harvest is conducted with a large, four-wheeled machine called a "car," which is driven along country lanes until a promising "roadside stand" is located. There, the desired fruits and vegetables are "picked up," boxed or bagged, and placed inside the vehicle, and a thick layer of "long green" is distributed by hand to insure a healthy production of crops in the coming year.

Hedge

Any of a number of fast-growing shrubs planted in a line as a fence or screen. Keeping them trimmed is a tricky and troublesome chore, and thus hedges are usually clipped by professionals—as are their owners.

Heeling In

Method of temporarily planting dormant rooted plants by placing them in a shallow trench dug with the back of the foot, then covering the roots with dirt. This technique suffers from the disadvantage that plants that are heeled in are more likely to die than those which are immediately planted in deep holes, but this drawback is more than compensated for by the ease with which they are disposed of when they do die.

Herbs

Widely grown and valuable plants useful as flavorings and preservatives. It's hard to agree on the most popular, but certainly a good candidate is sweet basil. The best-known variety is Rathbone basil, or wild Sherlock, a highly

Hose

aromatic plant on the basis of a very small whiff of whose pungent, peppery odor expelled from the oral cavity during speech, mingled with a hint of garlic, it is possible to deduce that the interlocutor has recently eaten Italian potato dumplings in a small cellar restaurant with a picture of the Bay of Naples on the wall.

Hoe

Gardening tool whose name derives from the fact that when its blade is stepped on, its handle delivers a sharp rap to the gardener's brow, at which point he cries "Ho!", or "Oh, ____!" or "Holy ____!"

Hollyhock

Tall flowering plant that has been nicknamed "the gardener's barometer" since it records high winds by falling over and breaking off near the ground, very heavy rain by losing all its blossoms, and the presence of Japanese beetles and the caterpillar stage of the rare painted-lady butterfly by disappearing entirely.

Honesty

Very attractive traditional plant with sweet-smelling purple-and-white flowers and papery seedpods. Some new varieties of this garden favorite are now available, including "Deniability," "Point-in-Time," "Best Recollection," and "Limited Immunity."

Hose

Crude, but effective and totally safe type of scythe towed through gardens to flatten flower beds and level vegetable plantings.

Houseplants

Quiet, good-natured, and very slow-moving pets, ideal for home or office environments. They are undemanding and good company, but don't approach them with excessive expectations. They are not likely to master more than the simplest of "tricks" ("sitting" and "playing dead" are just about it), and regardless of their size (and some ficuses and dracaenas can be real bruisers), they are not going to deter any but the most fainthearted and pusillanimous intruder, even where a "Beware of Plants" sign has been clearly posted in a conspicuous place.

Hydrangea   Strange behavior observed in gardeners during periods of heavy rainfall. Symptoms include obsessive tool care, irrational mail order purchases, the neurotic sorting of seed packets, and buying alcoholic beverages by the case.

Hydroponics   Rock and roll group that enjoyed a brief fad among gardeners in the 1950's after experiments at Cornell University suggested that popular music improved plant growth. Sales of their records dropped sharply when it was revealed that the growth effect, while valid, was essentially negative: An English ivy plant in the laboratory grew an astonishing 34 inches in 6 days, finally entwining itself around the tone arm of the record player, and a greenhouse orange tree managed to produce a four-pound fruit in one week, which it dropped on the turntable.

I

Impatiens   Fast-blooming flower. Plant it. Water it. It grows, it blooms. Bango, it makes seeds. It wilts. It dies. No hanging around for dirty tubers to form. No years of waiting for showy growth, fancy fruit. You got time on your hands, plant an acorn and lay in some Proust. You want quick results, impatiens is your baby.

Hydrangea (Type III: Irrational
Mail Order Purchases)

Insect

Insect	Insects are not "bad" by nature, but they quickly pick up antisocial habits by "hanging around" with thousands of "bad eggs" in crowded, dimly lit nests. (In more than one case, irresponsible mothers, or "queens," have been found to have over one million children—many more than they can care for properly.) It's a vicious cycle as newly hatched individuals get hooked on "plant juice" and turn into hardened garden felons. A few groups have tried working with insects. Arthropod House, for example, has had limited success retraining termites to sharpen pencils and has found jobs for some of the smaller flying insects in the circus field, but on the whole the picture is rather bleak.
Insecticides	A new respect for the environment and stricter regulations have taken most of the effective, but destructive, poisons off the shelf and replaced them with more benign, but less potent, compounds. Typical of the new insecticides are Annoyene, which gives some caterpillars a mild itching sensation; Migrene, which gives slugs a headache; and Dorene, Norene, and Charlene, a family of aromatic hydrocarbons based on inexpensive perfumes that have a vague repellent effect on grubs, chiggers, and mites.
Iris	Handsome, early-blooming perennial flower. Nowhere in botany are the remarkable genetic improvements of the last quarter-century more visible than among the irises. Most of the effort has gone into dramatically increasing the plant's size. With these developments comes, of course, the requirement for the modern gardener to equip himself with the new tools and accessories necessary for their cultivation and display. For example, to grow the leviathan iris (*I. godzilla*) with its huge, shade-producing blossoms and stately green trunk, the home gardener will want a bulb

winch, a stem ax, a 500-liter blossom tub, and—if he can afford it—one of those sporty gas-powered flower transporters. (A hard hat is also advisable—the petals on this hefty beauty weigh 20 pounds a piece!)

J

Jack-in-the-Pulpit   The state flower of Maryland. Shortly after being named, the designation was challenged by atheist groups who sued to have it removed on the constitutional grounds that its selection promoted religion. In a compromise that appears to have pleased no one, the plant was retained but officially renamed "Fred-in-a-phone-booth."

K

Key   *1.* Light, wing-shaped fruit from maple trees which, when dropped on the ground and buried under a shallow layer of soil, results in a new tree. *2.* Light brass or steel object which, when dropped on the ground and buried under a shallow layer of soil, results in a new padlock, a new hasp, and some new window glass.

Kudzu   Extraordinarily fast-growing vine accidentally introduced into the U.S., probably from China. There are the inevitable stories of kudzu plants growing in through open windows and suddenly grasping the unwary, but they must be apocryphal. No plant could possiblgll gckl gng—

Kudzu

Lawn (Improper Cutting Procedure)

Kumquat

Relative of citrus fruits long prized by comedians for its laughter-producing qualities. The most famous specimen is *Fructus risibilis johannes carsoni*, c.v. "Burbank Boffo."

L

Labyrinths, Mazes, and Knot Gardens

Intricate arrangements of shrubs, bushes, and other plants studded with statues and vases were striking highlights in 18th-century gardens. Alas, the creation of rigid geometric designs depends on an abundance of low-paid labor, and so in the 20th-century garden, eye-catching landscape elements simpler to achieve and maintain are preferred, particularly the Tangle, the Brushpile, the Overgrown Tire, and the Lone Cinderblock.

Lawn

Expanse of ground planted with one or more of a variety of grasses to produce a level, dense green cover with a uniform smooth appearance. Establishing and maintaining a lawn is not easy, but it is well within the competence of any reasonably dedicated gardener. The key to the process is a firm grasp of a few simple, straightforward principles of lawn building and care. The best book on the subject is the classic twelve-volume work, *A Brief Guide to Lawns*. Particular attention should be paid to the following chapters: "Drought—the Dread Lawn Killer"; "Overwatering—Grass Assassin"; "Daylight Sprinkling and Turf Burn"; "Nighttime Sprinkling and Turf Rot"; "Seed *vs.* Sod—the Gardener's Dilemma"; "Sun *vs.* Shade—the Impossible Balance"; and "The Case for Artificial Surfaces."

Leaf	The essential part of the basic plant cycle in which trees, shrubs, and bushes turn piles of dead leaves and branches into piles of dead branches and leaves.
Leggy	A plant is said to be "leggy" when it has a long, bare stem, and little foliage. Other undesirable characteristics include "pushy," "coarse," "rootless," "seedy," and "dead."
Legumes	Plants in the pea and bean families are able to obtain nitrogen directly from the atmosphere. These crops enrich the places where they are grown in two major ways: The portion of the plant remaining after the peas or beans are harvested can be plowed under; and gardeners with children can count on a sizable percentage of the peas and beans themselves being returned to the soil with their organic values intact, either by immediate transfer through a window or delayed distribution from pocket or napkin.
LeNotre	Celebrated 17th-century garden frog.
Lie	Common form of shorthand plant description used as a convenience by many nurseries.
Lilac	First introduced into America in the late 17th century, this fragrant flowering bush is now represented by over 500 varieties. Gardeners are often puzzled by their odd names. The explanation is simple: The vast majority of the great improvements in lilacs were made by the Lemoines in France, who, like so many other individuals of the era, were caught up in the impassioned politics of the 18th and 19th centuries, as a partial list of their more successful hybrids indicates: "Marie Antoinette" (1787); "Vive le Roi!" (1788); "A bas le Roi!" (1791); "Bastille" (1792); "Robespierre" (1794); "Mort a Robespierre!" (1795); "Napoleon" (1801); "Vive l'Empereur!" (1804); "Moscou" (1813); "A bas l'Em-

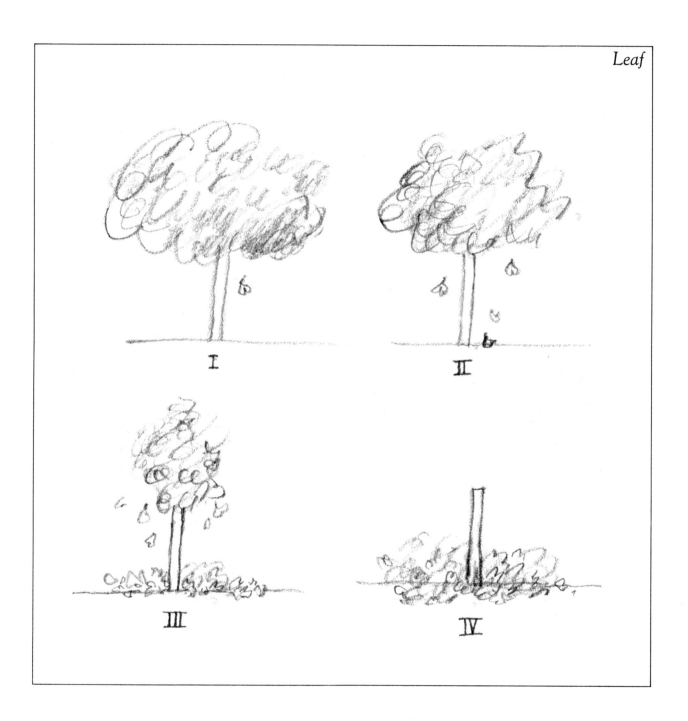

I

II

III

IV

Moon Planting

pereur!" (1814); "Vive l'Empereur Encore!" (1815); "Wellington" (1815); "Vive Louis XVIII!" (1817); "Vive la Revolution de Juillet!" (1830); "Vive Louis Philippe!" (1831); "Vive la Revolution de Fevrier!" (1848); "Napoleon II" (1852); "Mort a la Boche!" (1870); "Siegfried" (1870); "Vive la Republique!" (1874); "Sales Republicains!" (1876); "C'est la Vie" (1889); "Adieu Politique" (1890); "Vin Rouge" (1891); "Absinthe" (1894); "Pere Lachaise" (1895).

Lily of the Field	Attractive, unemployed, non-textile-producing flower.

M

Medicinal Plants	A number of plants have curious medicinal properties. Roses, for example, can cause severe headaches; lawn grasses have been known to produce an acute form of melancholy, and weeds may bring on muscular complaints.
Memorial Day Weekend	Traditional planting time in many northern parts of the country.
Monday After the Memorial Day Weekend	Traditional time to dig up and dispose of plants killed by unexpected hard frost the previous night.
Moon Planting	Some gardeners are convinced that vegetables do best if planted at a specific phase of the moon favorable for their development. There is no evidence that planting under a full moon either helps or hinders plant growth, but planting on the dark nights of the new moon and the early and late quarters can be injurious to seedlings as they may end up under a hedge, behind the garage, or in the driveway, the wading pool, or the barbecue pit.

Mulch	Material placed around the base of a plant to keep it moist and warm. Wood chips, leaf matter, and even old newspapers or other unwanted printed matter may be used. *(Note to the dissatisfied reader: The paper on which this book is printed has a high acid content and may damage plants.)*
Mushroom	Small room where vegetables are stored until they decompose into a pulpy mass suitable for the compost heap.
Myrrh	Menacing growling sound made by neighbor's dog just before attacking.
Myrtle	Peaceful gurgling sound made by neighbor's dog after having been fed a claw hammer.

N

Narcissus	Wonderful, early-blooming flower with an unsatisfactory plural form. Botanists have been searching for a suitable ending for years, but their attempts—narcissi (1947), narcissusses (1954), narcissus for both singular and plural (1958), and multinarcissus and polynarcissus (1962, 1963)—haven't enjoyed any real acceptance, and thus, gardeners still prefer to plant the easily pluralized daffodil or jonquil.
Nasturtium	Ancient Roman nose-bath sometimes used as an ornament in modern gardens. Similar to a birdbath, it consists of a heavy stone lid—the "septum"—in the center of which is the inhaling gate, or "sinusarium," a nose-size aperture that provides access to the "nostrilarium" itself, a deep water-filled bowl that traditionally contains watercress.

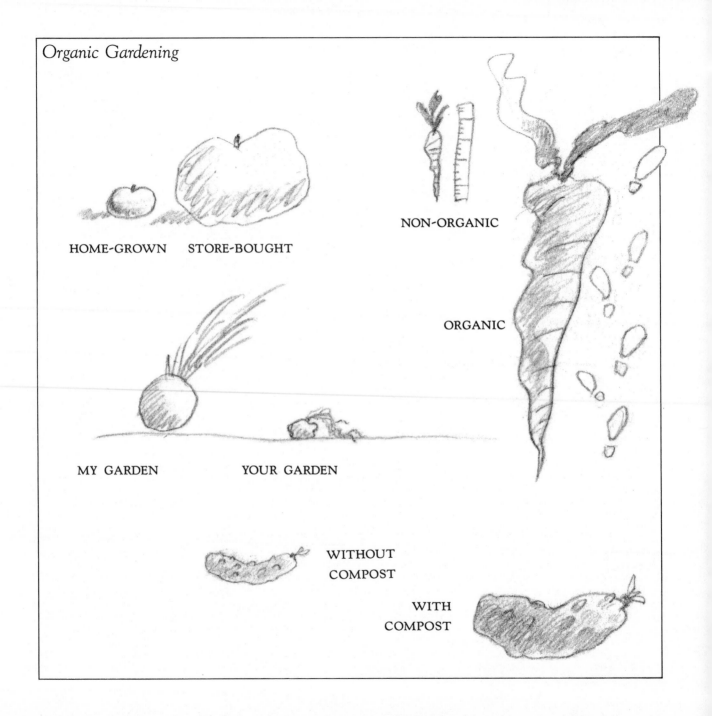

Organic Gardening

HOME-GROWN   STORE-BOUGHT

NON-ORGANIC

ORGANIC

MY GARDEN   YOUR GARDEN

WITHOUT
COMPOST

WITH
COMPOST

Naturalized

Any plant not native to this country that has escaped from a garden and established itself successfully in the wild is said to have become naturalized, and there are many of these new and not-so-new U.S. garden citizens around. With few exceptions, these newcomers have been warmly welcomed by American gardeners. Unhappily, however, there have been some black chapters in our horticultural history as well, most notably during World War I, when efforts were made to change "germination" to "Americanation" and several nasty incidents occurred in truck farms in the Northeast, during which sauerkraut cabbages were pelted with each other; and in World War II, when all the bonsai in the country were rounded up and put in a motel room in Eugene, Oregon.

Node

Portion of anatomy of hay fever sufferers most acutely affected by pollen in the atmosphere.

Nursery

The only known place where money grows on trees.

Nutshell

Handy container for abbreviated forms of botanical misinformation.

O

Organic Gardening

A gardening method in which, rather than being made the target of pesticides, insecticides, fungicides, and other chemicals, garden pests are controlled by being bored to death with excerpts from organic farming publications and texts. Most useful are *Characteristics of Soil Drainage in Loams and Gleys* (eliminates whitefly); *A History of Pectin* (excellent against rust and scale); *Comparative Nutritional*

Values of Bleached Nut Husks (effective against aphids); and *Determining Cesspool Gradients for Better Worm Culture* (chapters 47 through 54 are particularly good for maggot control).

Organizations

There are literally hundreds of horticultural groups in the U.S. There is only room here to include a brief list to give the reader a sense of the remarkable diversity of interests that have found expression in these botanical fraternities: American Society for the Propagation of Vines and Climbing Plants, c/o Warden, Ossining, N.Y.; American Cannabis Association, c/o "Freddy," Union Square, San Francisco, Calif.; The Society for Properly Blanched Plants, New Orleans, La.; The Ancient and Honorable Order of Hops, Barley, and Malt, South Boston, Mass.; Society for the Improvement of the Bean and Speedy Vehicles, Santa Monica, Calif.; National Association for the Promotion of Cauliflower as a Finger Food, New Hope, Pa.; Friends of Fungus, Luray Caverns, Va.; Ted's Cabbage Club, Bayonne, N.J.

Ornamental

A shrub, bush, or small tree that is transplanted at least twice in any calendar year.

P

Parasite

Anything in the garden that derives sustenance or energy from its host while providing nothing useful in return. Typical examples of parasitism include rechargeable electric grass clippers, small tractors, and melon plants.

Path

In most gardens, the shortest distance between two eyesores.

RIGHT

WRONG

Pest Control

Peaches and Pears — Everyone loves these trees, both for their fragrant flowers and their delicious fruit, but, alas, they are both afflicted with hundreds of diseases and disorders, including trunk drool, root slobber, bark slime, stemdrizzle, mush wood, limbsludge, twigfuzz, craptip, crud leaf, petal smudge, sprout droop, munge, dampcurl, bud custard, splotchblossom, devil's whiskers, lobe dropsy, creeping dinge, gray gange, bunkle, sperl, flenge, munge, morbisy, and snet. The only practical preventive measure is to dispose of young plants immediately by burning or burying.

Peat Moss — Organic substance used to keep soil loose and moist. One of the three things of interest to gardeners that Canada exports. The other two are cold air and black flies.

Perennial — Any plant which, had it lived, would have bloomed year after year. *See* ANNUAL.

Pest — Any creature that eats green vegetables without being compelled to.

Pest Control — The conventional method of dealing with pests involves the periodic application of small amounts of lead at very high velocities. It is somewhat effective in improving yields, but it limits the uses of the harvest to cole slaw, ratatouille, fruit cocktails, and dips.

Pheromone — Some success has been achieved in isolating the hormones given off by female insects for use in pest-control traps but fundamentalist Christians have blocked their sale in many places on the grounds that they promote "bug lust."

Philadelphus — Large, somewhat featureless white-flowered plant. It only has blossoms for about a week, but for some reason it seems more like a month.

Photosynthesis

A method of presenting specimens in the color photographs displayed in seed catalogs. The procedure involves the use of midgets and dwarfs to hold melons and stand by trees and the employment of a novel printing technique called Rhodogravure,™ in which the various vividly colored inks are applied directly to the flower or fruit before the actual photograph is taken.

Pinching

Pruning method developed in Italian gardens.

Pinks

A significant group of garden flowers, of which far and away the favorite is Sweet William. Lovers of this old-fashioned beauty will be happy to know that several new varieties are now available, including the rather dull but very hardy "Agreeable Roger"; the fast-spreading, almost weedlike "Boring George"; and for sour soils, the sturdy hybrids "Nasty Frank" and "Bitchy Susan."

Poison Ivy

If, like most people, you are allergic to this plant, the slightest touch is far worse than itching powder. You'll just have to learn to live with it—it's one of nature's little "gags." Others include lightning, floods, earthquakes, hurricanes, cobwebs, poodles, and the mumps.

Potato

The ideal vegetable. Potatoes are not bitter, not stringy, not pulpy, not sour, and not gritty. They are also not green, so tiresome nutritionists will say they are not "good" for you, but after all they *are* vegetables, not some sort of candy (although some of the sweet varieties can be easily transformed into something quite like a dessert). And boiling isn't the only thing you can do with them—they can be fried, baked, roasted, creamed, hash-browned, mashed, and rissoléed. Incredibly, they are even tasty served as a salad. And, best of all, since potatoes of excellent quality

Potato (Basic Types)

MAINE IDAHO TEXAS

are available everywhere the year round at very reasonable prices, there is absolutely no reason whatever to grow them—in fact, there is a very good reason not to.

Potato Beetle   The very good reason not to.

Prune   *1. (noun)* Disagreeable snack produced by placing plums in a lye solution, drying them for several weeks, then bathing them in glycerin. *2. (verb)* To selectively remove certain branches of a woody plant—for example, a plum tree—so that it will grow better and produce more fruit that can be made into an even larger quantity of disagreeable snacks.

Q

Quack Grass   *1.* Duck weed. *2.* Doc weed.

Quince   Fruit tree that lent its name to a traditional English garden sport. The game of quince is based on a wager in the late 14th century between the earl of Agway and the bishop of London as to whose gardeners could produce the first ripe quinces of the season to be made into jam for King Henry, who was very fond of the stuff. As it is played today, teams of amateur gardeners simultaneously plant specimens of the tree in barrels in the center of a quince court—a large greenhouse with seating for spectators. The object of the contest is deceptively simple: By careful pruning and the judicious use of precisely measured amounts of water, fertilizer, and plant sprays, to produce the first ripe quince weighing at least 7½ ounces. Modern matches, in a practice much deplored by traditionalists, start with mature trees rather than seed and last about 200 days, compared to the

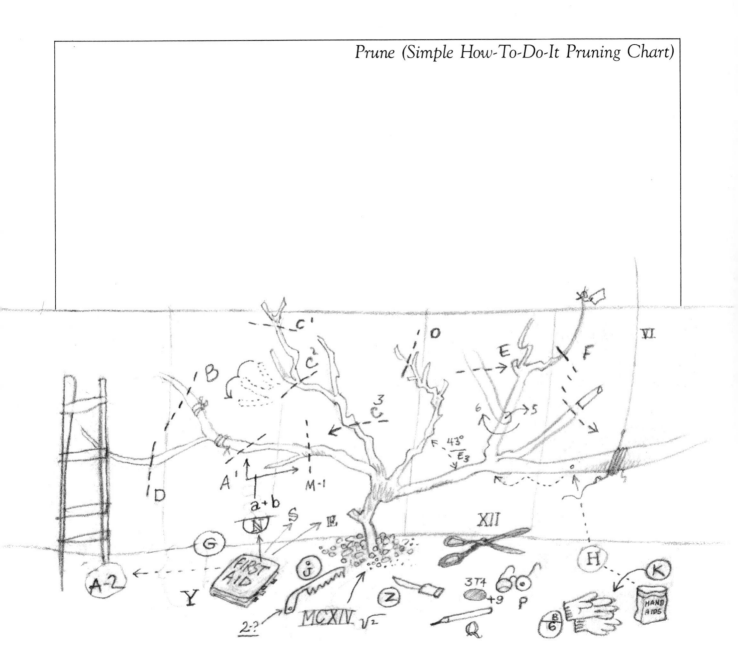

Rock Garden

four or more years of the prewar tussles. Attendance is generally spotty after the colorful opening ceremonies, but there are always a few people on hand to cry "good wood!" when a particularly well-thought-out bit of pruning is executed with a nice flourish of the shears. In the final week, the betting—not encouraged—is stiff, the tension is high, and the stands are packed as the judges begin to apply their scales to the larger fruits. And, of course, it is difficult to convey the excitement and the sheer drama in the center quince court at Kew in late September as the head judge plucks the winning fruit, mashes it with an ironwood gavel, and declares it "fit and worthy for His Majesty's muffins."

R

Rain	*See* WEEKEND.
Ranunculus	Third brother of Romulus and Remus. According to Roman legend, while his siblings were taken in and cared for by a she-wolf, Ranunculus was raised by buttercups. The shepherd who found Romulus and Remus stepped on Ranunculus, killing him instantly.
Rock Garden	An arrangement of rocks among which plants, chiefly alpine flowers, are placed. Alpines, as their name suggests, originate in the mountains, and it is the cool, dry, sunny weather of the upper altitudes that they prefer. Obviously, if they are to prosper in a less favorable environment, gardeners must try to convince them that they still *are* in the mountains, despite considerable evidence to the contrary, such as heat, smog, and heavy rains. Of course, putting

them in a rocky spot is a good start. Another effective trick is to wear a parka festooned with ski tags while working around them. Some gardeners also report success with a very simple expedient—placing a large sign advertising condominiums in a prominent location among the plants.

Roof Garden	Garden on a penthouse or terrace of an urban apartment. Because of increasingly harsh conditions in most cities, the only reliable products of roof gardens are the common house leak (*Gypsum discoloratum*) and the resulting rhubarb with the neighbor below.
Root	*1.* Subsurface part of a weed that is inadvertently left in the ground when the upper portion of the plant is removed, thus resulting in the weed's speedy regrowth. *2.* Subsurface part of an ornamental, or tree, a small portion of which is inadvertently left in the ground when the specimen is transplanted, thus resulting in the plant's rapid death.
Rose	There are thousands of hybrids of this beautiful and fragrant flower, but the most common type found in gardens is a specimen with a tight, 6-inch cluster of short, thick, brownish stems with large thorns, bearing a single shiny metal tag about 1½ inches in diameter.
Rosemary	There is some traditional quality associated with this plant, but the author regrets that he cannot, for the life of him, remember what it is.
Rot	Gardening advice.
Rotary Mower	Gasoline-powered metal detector used to locate misplaced trowels, shears, and hose nozzles in tall grass. The machine indicates a "contact" by giving off a loud *WHINNNNG!* sound, and then immediately stalling.

Scab, Scald, Scale, Scorch (Unfortunate Results Of)

Roto-tiller	Cultivating machine based on the principle of the raccoon.
Russian Olive	The hardy American hedgerow shrub is a non-fruit-bearing cousin of the true Russian olive (*Olea proletaria*, *c.v.* "Leafy Sidekick of the Working Classes"; *O. conspiratoria*, *c.v.* "Garden Plotter"; or *O. patriotica*, *c.v.* "Glorious Overproducer of Big Tasty Nuggets," depending on which edition of the *Soviet Botanical Encylopaedia* you consult). It grows only in one small stretch of the Black Sea coast to which it was banished by Stalin in 1946 after he became convinced that a specimen outside his window was responsible for his hay fever. (It was rehabilitated in 1957 and awarded the Hero of Socialist Fruit medal.) The fruit of the Russian olive, a globe about the size of a baseball with a 2-pound pit and hard gray flesh that tastes vaguely of creosote, is harvested by detonating high-explosive charges in orchards. The olives are then taken to presses and subjected to 20,000 p.s.i. of pressure, whereupon the fruit grudgingly yields about a quarter teaspoon of a thick, viscous oil, which is used as a cough syrup and gear lubricant.

S

Scab	Disorder in plants caused by fungi.
Scald	Disorder in plants caused by excessive sunlight.
Scale	Disorder in plants caused by sucking insects.
Scorch	Disorder in plants caused by drought.
Screaming Meemies	Disorder in gardeners caused by observing the effects of scab, scald, scale, and scorch.

Seed	Costly, but highly nutritious form of bird food sold in handsome packets printed with colorful pictures of flowers and vegetables.
Seed Tape	Novelty item sold as a practical joke to gullible gardeners who believe that rolls of adhesive tape are the fruit of a truly remarkable hybrid gum tree that can be grown in the garden.
Sequoia	Giant evergreen tree remarkable for its longevity and natural resistance to pests. Unfortunately, the very preservatives within its wood that render it invulnerable to all but one highly destructive pest have made its wood enormously desirable to that one pest for use in the construction of decks, hot tubs, planters, and lawn furniture, and for mulch chips.
Shakespeare Garden	Gardens containing every plant mentioned by Shakespeare have always had a certain popularity. Gardeners have looked to the contemporary theater for horticultural inspiration, but, alas, modern playwrights have proved a poor source of material: The only plants mentioned, for example, by Tennessee Williams are locoweed, moonseed, snakeweed, hellebore, persimmons, and sourberry; the only ones in Samuel Beckett's plays are vetch, gorse, bracken, and furze; and the sole citation of a botanical nature in a Eugene O'Neill drama is rye.
Shortest-lived Tree	The oldest trees—a giant redwood (about 4,000 years) and a bristlecone pine (over 7,000)—are well enough known, but the specimen with the briefest life span deserves wider notoriety. The generally accepted record for a transplanted tree is held by a 22-foot, $1,400 copper beech purchased in 1961 from a nursery in Delaware by Mr. W. E. Legett.

Soils

LOOSE SOIL HARD SOIL ACID SOIL ALKALINE SOIL

Thriving in its compact root ball when delivered, it died in an incredible four days, beating the previous record established by a magnolia in Kentucky by almost a full week.

Shrub-in-a-Tub
Those scraggly growths in concrete planters that line our city streets are a fascinating cross between a rare Finnish antler fungus and a native diet cherry. Their brittle, leafless branches in summer may convince the casual observer that they are as dead as an elm in Amsterdam, but the sharp-eyed botanist notices around their cracked and spotted trunks the telltale mounds of inch-long seedpods—so astonishingly like the filtertips of cigarettes—that mean these amazing plants are not only surviving, but thriving!

Snakes and Spiders
These two much-abused garden denizens are in fact helpful creatures with huge appetites for a wide array of animal and insect pests. Their frightening reputations are almost entirely undeserved, a point eloquently made by several distinguished biologists, including the recently deceased herpetologist, Dr. Phillip Morley (*Our Slithery Pals*); Mary Ann Cantwell, who managed in her tragically brief lifetime to produce the authoritative book, *The Muffet-Tuffet Syndrome—An Inquiry into Unreasonable Arachnophobia*; and C. T. Richard, whose massive three-volume opus, *So-called Poisonous Reptiles and Insects of North America* was completed, after his untimely death, by his gifted colleague, the late Ernst Dorffman.

Soils
There are basically three kinds of soil: sandy, clay, and loamy-muddy. How can you tell which type you have? Ask one of your children or a neighbor's child to come over and play in your yard. Inspect the results. Is it a castle, a tasteful little ashtray, or a messy mud pie? That's really all there is to it.

Sprinkler	Adjustable rotary irrigation device, typically with two settings: "Drool," which creates a puddle of water 6 inches deep in a circle about a yard in diameter, and "Monsoon," which propels a high-velocity water jet into the woods, the garage, your automobile, and the street.
Stake	Hard, somewhat tasteless garden product that generally constitutes the bulk of the harvest after visits by raccoons, groundhogs, rabbits, birds, squirrels, and deer.
Stump	*1.* Portion of a tree or large shrub remaining after removal of the trunk and branches. *2.* Portion of shovel remaining after using it in the attempted removal of *1.*
Sucker	According to the American Botanical Association, gardening is growing rapidly in popularity, with a potential new amateur gardener being born every sixty seconds!
Sundial	Ornamental garden clock that indicates the time by means of a shadow cast by a pointer onto a dial marked with numerals. Most sundials have inscriptions: The common ones are "Make Haste While the Sun Shines," "Tempus Fugit," and "Out of Order."

T

Tent Caterpillar	Destructive pest that eats leaves of affected trees—mainly apples and cherries. The best way to control them is to soak their sleeping bags with cold water, knock over their kerosene lanterns, and steal their tiny cans of Dinty Moore beef stew.

Terrarium

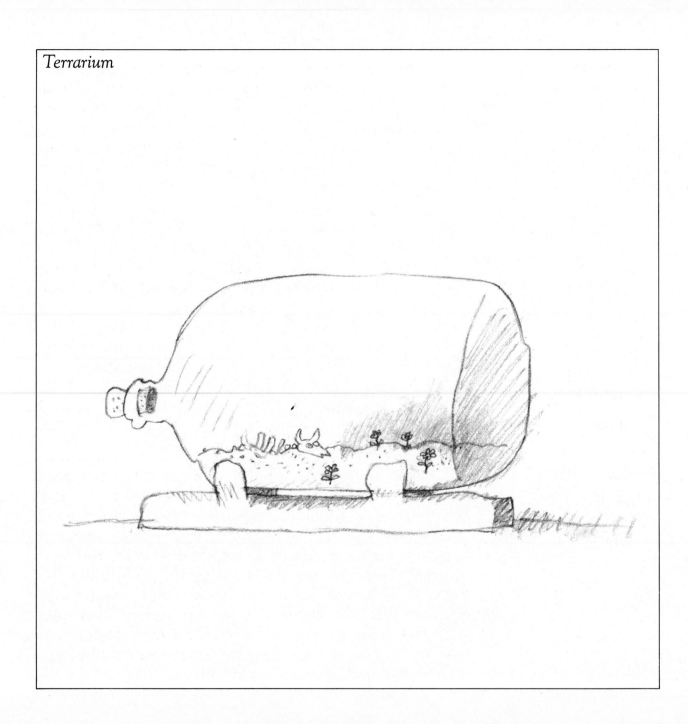

Terrarium	The home gardener who enjoys playing "God" can create a complete miniature closed environment in a covered jar, an old aquarium, or any other glass container. A balance of compatible plants and small animals, such as frogs or lizards, is essential. Once the little "world" is prospering, weird and contradictory "commandments" can be written on the backs of old dominoes or Scrabble tiles and dropped in through the top, while an old saucepan is beaten loudly with a spoon and the lights are turned on and off rapidly. Disappointment with the way things are going "down there" can be expressed by shaking the terrarium violently, as if preparing a whiskey sour; by "expelling" the inhabitants by turning it upside down; or by emptying a bucket or two of water into it along with vague plans for an "ark." And for an "end of the world" effect, it may be thrown from a second-story window or simply put in the garbage.
Toadstool	Ugly lawn furniture preferred by amphibians.
Tobacco	*1.* Delightful herb. *2.* Filthy Weed. *3.*Valuable crop. *4.* Foul growth. *5.* Source of discord among gardeners.
Tomato	This universally appreciated garden vegetable provides a fascinating demonstration of the biological "clocks" that all plants possess. Regardless of when tomatoes are planted, they will all become synchronized, mysteriously producing a gigantic crop of ripe fruit within a few hours of one another. This process can be triggered by "packing"—a method that entails making noisy and highly visible preparations for a trip, culminating in a dramatic "departure." The fruit will turn red and begin dropping to the ground within 15 or 20 minutes, and the harvest can usually begin after a few leisurely spins around the block.

Tools	Gardeners have long recognized that tools have a distinct life cycle just like anything else in the garden: active phase (1–12 weeks), marked by the appearance of telltale blisters on the hands and/or bruises on the legs of the user; metamorphosis phase (12–14 weeks), during which the handle suddenly breaks at the point where it is joined to the metal working end; and dormant phase (14 weeks–20 years), spent by the two halves of the tool resulting from metamorphosis, usually in a dark corner of a shed.
Topiary	The art of pruning and shearing plants so that they resemble animals. It is not as difficult to master as you might think. The key is the choice of subject. Avoid deer, swans, giraffes, and bears. Concentrate your efforts on depicting sponges, porcupines, frightened turtles, and sleeping hedgehogs.
Trace Elements	Many soils are deficient in one of the critical elements that plants require for nourishment. The following are the ones essential, together with their most common sources: iron (chip and till tricycles, roller skates, and small toys into soil); copper (dice and spread pennies); manganese (scatter shredded magnets); zinc (grind up and sow by hand faucets and French bistro decor); and molybdenum (distribute watch parts and knives).
Tree Paint	Tarry compound daubed on exposed tree wounds to prevent viruses and bacteria from penetrating the cambium layer, and usually smeared on hands, gloves, and clothes as well, possibly as a modern holdover from an ancient Druidic ritual in which the spirit of the tree, infuriated by having one of its favorite limbs hacked off to provide a little sunlight for the terrace, is propitiated and mollified by seeing the perpetrator of the deed covered in black goo.

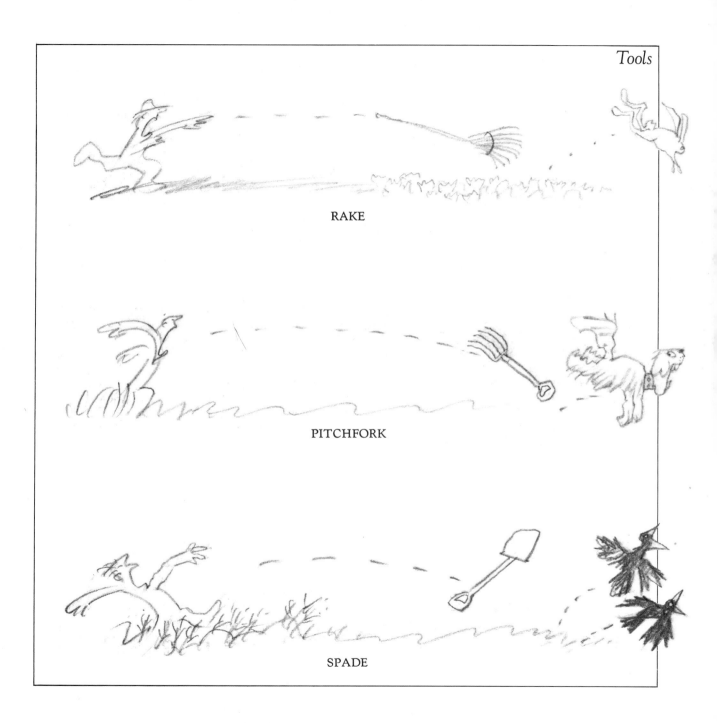

RAKE

PITCHFORK

SPADE

Tree Surgeon

Tree Surgeon	A house call by a "sawbranches" can be costly, but it is a good deal cheaper than transplanting a sick specimen to, say, the Cedars and Other Coniferous Evergreens of Lebanon Botanical Center in Los Angeles or the Infirmary at the Yale School of Forestry.
Trellis	Ladderlike structure along the side of a home designed for a climbing rose. Also suitable for a climbing rogue.
Tulip	Dutch blight second only to Dutch elm disease in severity. It affects most gardeners in late summer when it turns crisp green currency into shriveled brown bulbs that appear suddenly in mailboxes in early September. The only effective control method is to destroy the colorful pamphlets that spread the disease as soon as they appear. Under no circumstances should they be opened.
Tulip Tree	A large and striking flowering tree, often given as an Easter present in the late 1890's on Long Island's fabled Gold Coast. The cheerful chuffing of the steam tractors as they maneuvered the mammoth specimens in their giant pots and the creak of the winches as they deposited these massive plants in the conservatory announced the imminence of the long-awaited treasure hunt to eager children. The most lavish of these was held in 1899 at "Dunswindlin" in Glen Cove where a lucky young lad was the recipient of the Easter bunny's largesse—$85,000 in common stock of the American Chocolate Company.

U

Urned	What a peony saved sometimes is.

U.S. Department of Agriculture	Delightful organization that, in many cases, actually pays people not to grow things.

V

Vegetable	Many individuals are reluctant to raise animals for food, dreading as they do the inevitable emotional turmoil that accompanies the conversion of a pet into lunch. With members of the vegetable kingdom, it is easier to avoid attachments, but for the truly squeamish the harvest can be a trying experience. Here are a few hints that will make it easier to bear: Never talk to a plant you intend to eat; when digging up potatoes, avoid eye contact; do not pet soft-headed vegetables like lettuce and cabbage; don't give your melons and pumpkins names; and always apply fertilizer with a mechanical dispenser rather than by hand.
Vermiculite	Obscure order of nuns dedicated to gardening. Like other devotional orders, the sisters take the traditional vows of chastity, poverty, and obedience, but in keeping with the demanding nature of their calling, the Vermiculites are the only such group with a special dispensation to drink, smoke, swear, and throw things.
Viburnum	P. T. Viburnum, master flower showman. Highlights of his spectacular botanical extravaganzas included William Ward Hitchcock III's Wild Flowers of the West Show with "authentic specimens of grasses and blossoms obtained from the O.K. Corral"; Gertrude Oakley Foster, who arranged flowers on horseback; and a sideshow featuring a collection of malformed squashes.

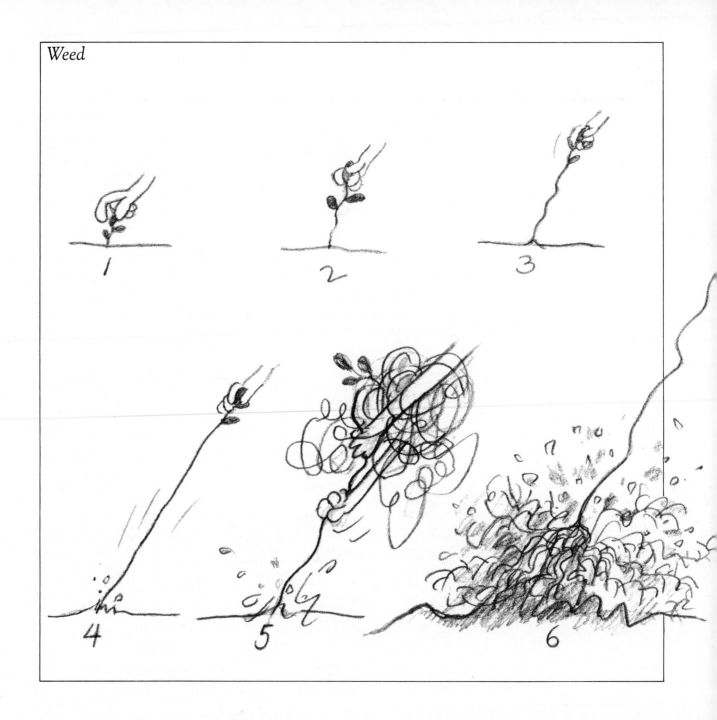

W

Wasps

Annoying pests deliberately introduced into much of North America from England during the 16th, 17th, and 18th centuries. They have infested large areas of the U.S. and Canada, destroying millions of acres of lush forests and verdant plains and replacing them with their preferred habitat, a mixture of boxy dwellings, telltale spired religious structures, and desertlike golf courses. Characterized by a low-pitched drone, an antlike industriousness, and extremely perfunctory mating behavior, they can generally drink their own weight in fermented liquids in a day. No method of dislodging them has ever been found.

Water

Gardens obtain vital moisture in three ways: from the atmosphere, through precipitation or condensation; from reservoirs, through irrigation; and from gardeners, through perspiration and lacrimation.

Weed

Any plant that will survive at least one week without being watered, fertilized, pruned, sprayed, staked, mulched, misted, dusted, or wrapped in burlap, paper, or plastic.

Weekend

See RAIN.

Weights and Measures

Gardeners have to contend with a number of weights and measures. Here is a conversion table for the ones most commonly encountered.

GRASS SEED:	LIQUIDS:
1 pound = 11 ounces	1 nip = ¼ draught
1 sq. ft. = 88 sq. in.	1 slug = 19 drams
PESTICIDES:	FENCE HEIGHT:
1 beetle = ½ bottle	1 hop = 2 skips
1 hornet = 22 spritzes	2 skips = 1 jump

Wheelbarrow	Mobile birdbath.
Willow	Picturesque but weak tree with brittle branches, a fatal susceptibility to insect pests, and a shallow root system. *Salix babylonica*, the classic weeping willow, is the best known and most extensively planted of the species, but two new varieties are achieving some popularity: *S. materna*, the suffering willow, a short, somewhat dumpy tree that prefers full sun but doesn't mind being in the shade as long as all the other trees are comfortable; and *S. lachrymosa*, the whining willow, a low-growing shrub that will survive almost anywhere but would have done much better if it had had the opportunities and attention that some of the more favored trees and bushes received.

X

X.	Botanical symbol for a hybrid or cross between two existing varieties. Nurseries often cross plants to produce a new one with desirable characteristics from each of the progenitors. Thus, for example, a small, rare, ugly, slow-selling shrub with a $29.95 price tag might be crossed with a large, showy, common flower with a $4.95 price tag to produce a large, showy, common shrub with a $39.95 price tag.

Y

Yard	*1. (penology)* Dusty open area where hard labor is performed. *2. (horticulture)* Dusty open area where hard labor is performed.
Yes	Nurseryman's term for "no."

Yard

Zones (Northern)

Z

Zones	The most widely used climate maps divide North America into ten different zones, but for practical purposes there are really only two: those areas where frost is the major concern and those where the major concern is Spanish-speaking neighbors.
Zucchini	The only garden vegetable with its own ZIP code.
Zzzz	*1.* Sound produced by dozing gardener. *2.* Sound produced by bee trapped in dozing gardener's pants leg.